W9-CHR-679

BLACK BEARS

PowerKiDS
press

New York

Meryl Magby

Published in 2014 by The Rosen Publishing Group, Inc.
29 East 21st Street, New York, NY 10010

First Edition

Editor: Amelie von Zumbusch
Book Design: Ashley Drago
Layout Design: Colleen Bialecki

Photo Credits: Cover James Gritz/Photodisc/Getty Images; p. 5 Tom Reichner/Shutterstock.com; p. 6 Wyatt Rivard/Shutterstock.com; p. 7 iStockphoto/Thinkstock; p. 8 aim/Shutterstock.com; p. 9 Lana Lanlois/Shutterstock.com; p. 10 Jupiterimages/Photos.com/Thinkstock; p. 11 Mighty Sequoia Studio/Shutterstock.com; pp. 12–13 Dave Skinner/E+/Getty Images; p. 14 Wayne Lynch/All Canada Photos/Getty Images; p. 15 John Serrao/Photo Researchers/Getty Images; p. 16 Scenic Shutterbug/Shutterstock.com; p. 17 iStockphoto/Thinkstock; p. 18 Altrendo Nature/Altrendo/Getty Images; p. 19 Robert Caputo/Aurora/Getty Images; p. 20 Thomas O'Neil/Shutterstock.com; p. 21 IDAK/Shutterstock.com; p. 22 Mike Rogal/Shutterstock.com.

Library of Congress Cataloging-in-Publication Data

Magby, Meryl.
  Black bears / by Meryl Magby — First edition.
      pages cm. — (American animals)
  Includes index.
  ISBN 978-1-4777-0791-3 (library binding) — ISBN 978-1-4777-0954-2 (pbk.) —
ISBN 978-1-4777-0955-9 (6-pack)
  1. Black bear—Juvenile literature. I. Title.
  QL737.C27M248 2014
  599.78′5—dc23
                                                2013000198

Manufactured in the United States of America

CPSIA Compliance Information: Batch #S13PK6: For Further Information contact Rosen Publishing, New York, New York at 1-800-237-9932

Contents

Smart Bears

American black bears are smart, **curious** animals. They are known for their amazing sense of smell, which helps them find food. They are also known for climbing trees. Sometimes black bears make a mess of people's campsites, yards, and homes. This is because they are looking for human food or garbage to eat.

> American black bears are quite common. There are more American black bears than all of the other kinds of bears in the world put together!

American black bears are **native** to North America, as are brown bears and polar bears. Black bears are the smallest of the three bears that live in North America. However, they are also the most common. The American black bear's closest relative is the Asian black bear.

Only in North America

Wild American black bears live only in North America. They can be found throughout Canada, the United States, and parts of northern Mexico. However, black bears are less common in Midwestern states than they are in other parts of the United States. Scientists think there are between 850,000 and 950,000 black bears in North America.

Alaska has the more black bears than any other state. Washington, Oregon, California, Idaho, Minnesota, Wisconsin, and Maine also have large numbers of these bears.

Black bears live in **habitats** with many trees and shrubs. These include forests, swamps, and wetlands throughout North America. Black bears need to live in places that have lots of plants to eat and water to drink. They often live near lakes and rivers.

Black bears like water. They can swim for at least 1.5 miles (2.4 km) in freshwater.

Paws and Claws

Most, but not all, black bears have black fur. The fur around their **muzzles** is brown. Some black bears have a patch of white fur on their chests. Adult black bears are about 6 feet (2 m) long from nose to tail. Male bears generally weigh about 300 pounds (136 kg). Females weigh about 160 pounds (73 kg).

When they are standing on all four paws, adult black bears are about 3 feet (1 m) tall at the shoulder.

Black bears have five toes on each of their four paws. Each toe has a curved claw that is 2 inches (5 cm) long. These claws make it very easy for black bears to quickly climb trees. Black bears are also good swimmers!

Living Alone

Black bears are mostly **solitary**. However, mother bears live with their babies. Each bear has an area in which it finds dens and looks for food, called a **home range**. Male bears' home ranges are much larger than those of females. When there is not much food to share, bears may become territorial. This means they try to keep other bears out of their home ranges.

Standing up on its hind, or back, legs gives this black bear a chance to get a better look at something.

In Florida, male black bears' home ranges cover between 50 and 120 square miles (129–311 sq km). Those of females are between 10 and 25 square miles (26–66 sq km).

Black bears **communicate** with sounds, smells, and markings. The sounds bears make include whines, coughs, snorts, sniffs, growls, and woofs. Bears mark trees by biting them and scratching them with their claws. They also mark their ranges with **urine** and droppings.

Black Bear Facts

1. Most black bears have black fur. However, their fur can sometimes be other colors. In North America, you can find black bears with dark brown, light brown, or even white fur!

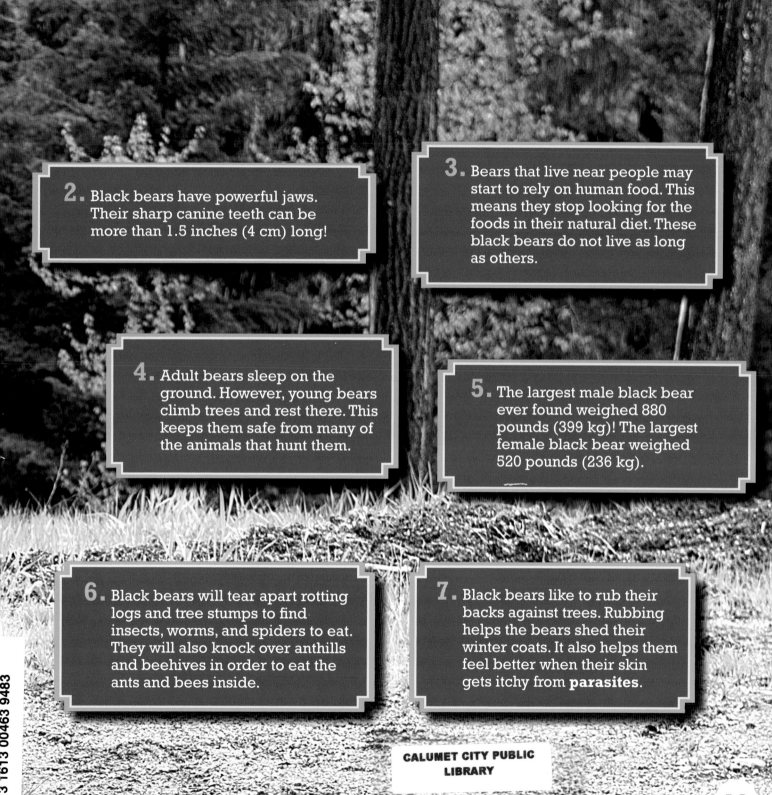

2. Black bears have powerful jaws. Their sharp canine teeth can be more than 1.5 inches (4 cm) long!

3. Bears that live near people may start to rely on human food. This means they stop looking for the foods in their natural diet. These black bears do not live as long as others.

4. Adult bears sleep on the ground. However, young bears climb trees and rest there. This keeps them safe from many of the animals that hunt them.

5. The largest male black bear ever found weighed 880 pounds (399 kg)! The largest female black bear weighed 520 pounds (236 kg).

6. Black bears will tear apart rotting logs and tree stumps to find insects, worms, and spiders to eat. They will also knock over anthills and beehives in order to eat the ants and bees inside.

7. Black bears like to rub their backs against trees. Rubbing helps the bears shed their winter coats. It also helps them feel better when their skin gets itchy from **parasites**.

Sleeping All Winter

Black bears do not truly **hibernate** during the winter, as some mammals do. However, they do find dens and spend most of the cold months sleeping there. Black bears enter their dens in the fall, before cold winter weather starts. A den could be a hollow tree or log, a space between two large rocks, or a hole dug in the ground.

This mother black bear is sleeping in her winter den as her baby looks on.

Black bears choose small spaces for their dens. The bears lose less body heat in small spaces. This keeps them warm while they rest. Black bears do not eat or drink in their winter dens. Instead, they use stored body fat for energy.

Black bears will lose as much as 40 percent of their body weight while they are sleeping in their winter dens.

Curious Bear Cubs

Black bears **mate** during the spring and summer. Female bears give birth in their winter dens. The babies are called cubs. They are blind and weigh less than 1 pound (.5 kg). They drink their mother's milk and grow quickly. Mother bears and their cubs leave the den in late spring. By then, the cubs weigh about 10 pounds (5 kg).

Black bear mothers generally have 2 or 3 babies at a time.

Cubs are curious. They like to play and wrestle with their brothers and sisters. Cubs stay with their mothers until they are about a year and a half old. Black bears can live to be about 30 years old in the wild.

A black bear cub's mother teaches it how to find food and climb trees.

Plants and Animals

Black bears are **omnivores**. This means they eat both plants and animals. However, their diet is mostly plants. Some of their favorite foods are berries, fruits, nuts, roots, grasses, insects, and fish. However, black bears are also known for eating human food, pet food, crops, and garbage left out by people.

Black bears are drawn to human food. Campers in areas where these bears live should always store food in airtight containers. Coolers are not a good choice!

Berries are an important part of most black bear diets. Black bears eat many kinds of berries, including blueberries, raspberries, juneberries, blackberries, and huckleberries.

Black bears have an amazing sense of smell. Scientists think that they can smell food from more than 1 mile (1.6 km) away! Sometimes they stand up on their hind legs to find smells better. Black bears see in color. This helps them see fruits and berries growing on bushes.

Black Bear Predators

In some places where they live, black bears are at the top of the food chain. This means that they have no animal **predators**. However, sometimes adult black bears are killed by grizzly bears or other black bears. Coyotes and mountain lions will hunt black bear cubs. Cubs are easier to catch than adults. They are much smaller and slower than adult black bears.

Many states that allow black bear hunting permit it only during set hunting seasons.

Black bears have often been hunted for their thick fur. People make bear rugs out of black bear fur and skin. Bearskin has been used to make hats, too.

Humans also hunt black bears. Native American peoples have long hunted black bears for their meat and fur. European settlers started hunting bears when they arrived in North America. Today, black bears are hunted for sport in many states.

Not in Danger

Black bears are very common in North America. They are not in danger of dying out any time soon. In fact, the number of black bears is growing in the United States and Canada! These bears are finding new places to live, as forests grow back in place of farmland in some parts of North America.

If you see a black bear while you are outdoors, do not get too close. Black bears have been known to attack people. However, this is generally when they are trying to get at someone's food.

Black bears are making a comeback in many states, including New Hampshire, New Jersey, Pennsylvania, and Arkansas.

Glossary

communicate (kuh-MYOO-nih-kayt) To share facts or feelings.

curious (KYUR-ee-us) Interested in new things.

habitats (HA-buh-tats) The kinds of land where an animal or a plant naturally lives.

hibernate (HY-bur-nayt) To spend the winter in a sleeplike state.

home range (HOHM RAYNJ) The area in which an animal usually stays.

mate (MAYT) To join together to make babies.

muzzles (MUH-zelz) The parts of animals' heads that come forward and include the noses.

native (NAY-tiv) Born or grown in a certain place or country.

omnivores (OM-nih-vawrz) Animals that eat both plants and animals.

parasites (PER-uh-syts) Living things that live in, on, or with other living things.

predators (PREH-duh-terz) Animals that kill other animals for food.

solitary (SAH-leh-ter-ee) Spending most time alone.

urine (YUR-un) A liquid waste made by the body.

Index

Websites

Due to the changing nature of Internet links, PowerKids Press has developed an online list of websites related to the subject of this book. This site is updated regularly. Please use this link to access the list:

www.powerkidslinks.com/amer/bear/